WHAT WILL YOU GIVE ME FOR A FIVER?

YOU TIGHT GIT

£5

JAKE HARRIS

With illustrations by Sarah Arnold

summersdale

WHAT WOULD YOU DO FOR A FIVER?

Summersdale Publishers Ltd
46 West Street
Chichester
West Sussex
PO19 1RP
UK

www.summersdale.com

Printed and bound in Great Britain
ISBN: 978-1-84953-093-4

Substantial discounts on bulk quantities of Summersdale books are available to corporations, professional associations and other organisations. For details contact Summersdale Publishers by telephone: +44 (0) 1243 771107, fax: +44 (0) 1243 786300 or email: nicky@summersdale.com.

DISCLAIMER

This book is intended for entertainment purposes only and it is not recommended that readers actually engage in any of the ridiculous, nauseating and at times downright dangerous actions described. The publisher cannot accept any responsibility for any loss, damage, psychological trauma, social alienation, complete loss of self-respect, injury or death caused by partaking in activities represented in this book.

FOR A FIVER, WOULD YOU...

... lick a dirty old tramp?

... do a commando roll into your weekly staff meeting before walking to your chair calmly as if nothing had happened?

... snort a line of mustard powder?

... PICK SOMEONE ELSE'S NOSE AND EAT THE BOGIE?

... buy a bargain bucket of fried chicken, eat the lot, then take it back for a refund, claiming it had a bone in it?

... give your friends your Facebook password?

... replace the first letter of most words you say with a 'B' for a day? For example: 'I'm boing to the bovies to watch a bilm.'

... creep around in the style of a pantomime villain and shout 'HE'S BEHIND YOU!' in the ears of unsuspecting people?

... sit at the back of a bus and make loud clucking sounds, then after two minutes drop a hard-boiled egg so that it rolls down the central aisle?

... shout 'For the love of Moses, NO!'
whenever you hear the words 'I'm just
popping to the shops' for a week?

... wear leather trousers
and braces to work?

... hug your friend tightly, making sure that
your hair touches for a couple of moments,
before scratching your head frantically
and saying that you have a really bad case
of nits that you can't seem to get rid of?

... sing 'Cry Wolf' by a-ha every time the phone rings – including at work?

... moon the drivers on your nearest main road at rush hour?

... eat a slice of bread that has been rubbed under a really sweaty person's armpit? (There is an extra quid in it if you consume any stowaway underarm fluff.)

... dry hump a bollard on a busy
street for a minute?

... give yourself five paper cuts?
(One pound for each cut.)

... use old, lumpy milk to make everyone
in your house a vanilla milkshake, passing
off the lumps as thick bits of ice cream?

... end every sentence with 'meeeeow' for a week?

... wash your hair with rotten eggs?

... go into the changing room of a designer shop and come back out with your clothes on inside out? You have to spend ten minutes browsing before you leave.

WOULD YOU PUT A CIGARETTE BUTT UP YOUR NOSE FOR £8.70?

... spend ten minutes in the toilet of your local pub making groaning sounds before emerging with an exhausted but relieved look? (An extra five pounds is up for grabs if you provide a running commentary to the person in the next cubicle.)

... strap on a pregnancy pillow and pretend to be pregnant for a day, announcing to everyone you meet that your nipples 'are feeling sore today'?

... perform 'I'm a Barbie Girl' on karaoke night at your local pub?

FOR A TENNER, WOULD YOU...

... slap yourself in the face every hour on the hour for a day?

... speak using only the phrase 'A-shadappa-ya-face!' for a week?

... call your in-laws for a chat while taking a shit? You can't lie about what you are doing if asked.

... TAKE A SHOT OF VODKA THROUGH YOUR EYE?

... put itching powder on a toilet roll, use it yourself and then leave it there for the next person?

... shout 'clunge' at the top of your voice in the cinema during kids club on a Saturday morning?

... go up to someone who is chewing gum and ask them if you can have it when they're finished for your 'art installation'? If they say yes and hand it over, put it in your own mouth and run off shrieking hysterically.

... stuff your trousers (or bra) with enough socks to make a hefty bulge, then draw attention to the area by continually complaining how it's feeling really tight today?

... clip off your toenails, put them in a sandwich and then eat it? It has to be a basic bread and butter sandwich – no sauces or toppings allowed!

... sit on an old man's lap and tell him you'll be his toy boy/playgirl?

... do a striptease in the middle of the dance floor at your local club and keep going until you get stopped?

... dress up as a baby, including a huge nappy, dummy and bonnet, and then chase every busty girl you see in the street, wailing 'MILK MUMMY, MILK!'?

... put on your mum's bra and walk down the street singing 'I'm too sexy for my shirt'?

... shave yourself using vinegar instead of shaving foam?

... powder your arse cheeks with blusher, wear a 'mankini' and ask strangers to rub your bottom with a dock leaf, saying you've fallen in a patch of stinging nettles?

... EAT A SLUG?

... crush ten beer cans with your bare feet?

... fill a stranger's shopping trolley with Vaseline and phallic-shaped vegetables?

... gulp down a mixture of off milk, fish paste and over-cooked, mashed-up Brussels sprouts? You have to drink a whole pint – if you're sick you have to start again.

... use red food dye and chocolate to create interesting stains on some old underwear, then take it down to your local charity shop and ask if they will accept soiled goods?

... make all your limbs go dead and try to walk on all fours?

FOR £20, WOULD YOU...

... send an email to all of your work colleagues that shows a photo of your arse with a plastic alien stuck to it, bearing the caption 'Is there life on M'ars?'?

... smoke a tampon outside the pub?

... tell all your mates you're a virgin and have become an ambassador for True Love Waits?

... scrape a piece of gum off the underside of a desk, park bench or bus seat and chew it for five minutes?

... throw an egg in a complete stranger's face and then carry on walking down the road as if nothing has happened? An extra five pounds if you utter the awful pun 'The yoke's on you' before walking off.

... DRESS AS A VICAR AND SKATEBOARD THROUGH TOWN?

... casually mention to one of your friends or work colleagues that you had a thoroughly enjoyable sex dream involving them, a Womble and twelve cans of Heinz Spaghetti Hoops?

... arrange a dinner party and, after filling everyone's glass and proposing a toast, ask how your guests are enjoying their piss spritzer and go on to explain the health merits of drinking urine?

... draw a cartoon penis on every piece of paperwork that you come across at work?

... at the suggestion of a staff pancake day send a mass email saying, 'That's a good idea, there are definitely some tossers in this company'? There is an extra £50 if during the event you look at a colleague and say, 'You're one of 'em!'

... get dressed up as an American redneck and attend your local political candidate's rally, then in the middle of their speech on unemployment scream in a southern drawl 'They took our jobs!!!!'?

... sit on a crate in your local supermarket for an hour, dressed in a leotard, with a 'buy me' sign around your neck? If anyone shows an interest, you have to haggle for the best price.

... in the middle of winter, pull down your pants and sit on an icy bench? If your butt gets stuck, you have to stay put until there is a thaw.

... wait on the other side of a swinging door until someone comes along to push it open and into your face?

... toast your fingers?

... rent a Bigfoot costume and spend a day lurking in the gardens in your neighbourhood, occasionally shouting 'I am the Yeti!'?

... jump onto a stranger rodeo style and attempt to cling on for two minutes?

... put a light bulb in your mouth?

... build a lingerie fort in Marks and Spencer and launch an assault on customers by pinging elasticated knickers at them?

FOR £25, WOULD YOU...

... replace your face powder with powdered parmesan and wear your new make-up for a night on the town?

... cover yourself in superglue and dive into a pile of leaves?

... attach a fox's tail to your bottom before going to work and lick the tail every time someone comes to talk to you, as if preening yourself?

... EAT A LIVE GOLDFISH?

... wipe your bum with sandpaper?

... say in your best camp voice 'mince, mince, mince' every time your boss walks past your desk?

... wear loose-fitting trousers to the pub and fill your pants with Cheestrings, then whip one out mid-conversation to munch on and offer them round to your friends?

... spend an afternoon reading at your local library with a condom on your head?

... make a skirt out of newspaper, wear it to work, then eat a portion of chips directly off it at lunchtime? You have to leave the grease-sodden garment on for the rest of the day.

... allow a friend to test their new Taser gun on you?

... wear extra-long fake nails for a week and whenever asked a question, tap your nails on your chin as if contemplating the answer and say: 'I think you've hit the nail on the head with that question'?

... gather up a load of guinea pig poos, coat them in chocolate, mix them into a packet of Revels and offer them to your mates, saying there is a new secret flavour and it's bloody lovely? An extra £25 if you can get a mate to down the entire packet.

... jump off a diving board at the public swimming pool during the mid-morning rush to perform a belly flop while yelling, 'I am the human fish! WATCH ME DIVE CHUMPS!!!'?

... have your hair styled into a mullet and adopt 'Business up front, party at the back' as your chat-up line for a month?

... give yourself a Tabasco facemask?

... LEAVE YOUR FLIES OPEN FOR THE MORNING AT WORK WITH YOUR OLD CHAP HANGING OUT?

... coat your tongue in nail
polish and let it dry?

... tape ten beers to your hands,
and only remove the empty cans
when you've drunk them all?

... sunbathe on a hot day with the shape
of an inverted pentagram drawn in
super-strength sunblock on your chest?

FOR £50, WOULD YOU...

... dye your underarm hair orange and wear sleeveless tops for two weeks?

... email all your exes and tell them that you're still in love with them?

... take a shit in your front garden?

... carry a couple of trout in your trouser pockets for a day and ask everyone you meet 'What's that fishy smell? Gees... you need to wash more!'?

... wear white contact lenses so it looks like you have no irises or pupils and walk with a limp through town going 'Arrrrggggghhhh!' at everyone?

... tell all your friends that you've won the lottery and let them buy you pints and dinners for a week before telling the truth?

... LET A SPIDER CRAWL ACROSS YOUR TONGUE?

... after agreeing to meet your partner's parents, turn up on the day with a home-made sock puppet named Dave and claim that you're all involved in a three-way sexual relationship?

... wear a lab coat, go up to a dog walker and ask them if it would be all right to collect their dog's fresh turd for 'scientific purposes'? When you've finished asking the question, you must lick your lips and collect the specimen with your bare hands.

... make a batch of cat food pies for a party and tell your guests that they are beef and onion? For £500, make the pies with cat shit.

... shave your head completely and if anyone asks why, tell them you heard Right Said Fred were getting back together and you're auditioning to be a new member?

... collect a month's worth of dry skin shavings from a crusty old man's feet in an empty gourmet crisp packet, then offer your boss one to try at the annual work picnic?

WOULD YOU GLUE ALL YOUR HAIR
TOGETHER AS ONE MASSIVE
DREADLOCK AND TELL EVERYONE
YOU WILL FROM NOW ON BE KNOWN
AS 'THE BEAVER' FOR £65.90?

... apply four bottles of fake tan and don a Rasta wig to attend a wedding?

... handcuff yourself to a complete stranger and tell them that you can't find the key? You must stay cuffed to them for five minutes or longer.

... arrive at work one morning wearing your underwear outside your clothes? For an extra £10, wear them inside out with skid marks on show.

... smother fish paste over someone's crotch and lick it all off?

... offer to give your best mate's grandmother a blue rinse down below to match her new hair-do?

... change your Facebook status to an admission of a particularly persistent STD? You may not post a retraction.

FOR £50, WOULD YOU...

... PULL UP AT THE PETROL STATION, OPEN YOUR PETROL CAP AND PROCEED TO PEE INTO THE TANK, EXPLAINING THAT THEY'VE RUN OUT OF FOUR STAR IF ANYONE ASKS WHY?

... phone in sick, saying you can't come in because you've an intimate body part stuck in the vacuum cleaner AGAIN?

... bleach your eyebrows and recreate Spock's eyebrows in permanent pen?

... play 'Roxanne' by The Police and drink a tequila shot every time Sting sings her name? You don't have time to do salt and lemon.

... rub ten bird's-eye chillies in your eyes?

... pull a hairball out of the bathroom drain with your teeth?

... put your tongue in an electric fan?

... rip off one of your fingernails?

... open your front door just as the postman is approaching, bend over and say 'Just stick it in the slot, please'?

FOR £100, WOULD YOU...

... dine on pigs' ears and dormice for a week, saying it's the new medieval diet?

... shave off all your pubes and stick them to your face for a Saturday night out on the town?

... French kiss your dog for a minimum of 30 seconds?

... have your face painted as Mickey Mouse (complete with the ears) to attend a relative's christening? If anyone asks why you must respond, 'I bloody love that mouse.'

... wear a tutu to the office and perform lunges in front of your boss's desk?

... go to the police station and claim that while you were out sunbathing you had been raped by a huge badger?

... perform a naked bar streak?

... punch your mum in the face?
£200 if you punch your nan.

... wear a superhero outfit made out of a
brown unitard with a big label saying 'Super
Duper Diarrhoea Man' across your chest?

... START AND LOSE A FIGHT WITH A FAT GRANNY?

... take Viagra before walking naked through a packed nudist beach, saying 'Hi!' to everyone in a big voice, and a tiny 'Hi!' from your willy?

... spend your lunch break at your computer, gradually removing all but your underwear, and claim that you suffered a crushing defeat in your online strip poker league?

... attempt the world record for wearing the most pairs of pants at once? (They must be pre-worn by other people and unwashed.)

... put on your Facebook page: 'I may be out of touch for a couple of weeks while I have sexual re-assignment surgery. I will let you know my new preferred name if all goes OK. Wish me luck.'?

... cup a random bloke's balls in the street?

... watch every single one of the 365 episodes of *Teletubbies* back to back? You may not sleep for the duration, and can only eat custard and toast.

———

... very realistically pretend to reach orgasm in the back of a cinema in the middle of a film?

WOULD YOU EAT AN APPLE KNOWING THERE WAS A LIVE MAGGOT IN IT FOR £130.27?

... get dressed up as Gollum from *Lord of the Rings* and squat in the high street with a pack of Hula Hoops, nursing each one gently and saying 'Ah, my precious!' before gobbling it down?

... pretend to have a violent seizure in a public place, and when someone rushes over to help stop abruptly and hand them a flyer for a local 'alternative' dance class?

... go to your local pub quiz with a box of out-of-date eggs and smash one on top of your head every time you get a question wrong?

... cover yourself in spray mount and attempt to attach yourself to the wall? If you succeed, you must stay stuck there until someone comes to peel you off.

—

... give up speaking for an entire week, and communicate by writing messages on your skin?

—

... get dressed up in a trench coat, fake moustache and thick glasses, then hang out at the local playground with a camera round your neck, rubbing your crotch and grunting, 'Would you like some sweeties boys and girls?'

... agree to be tied to a chair and hit repeatedly with snooker cues by friends and family to the tune of 'Don't Stop Me Now' (like in *Shaun of the Dead*)?

... chew a hairy mole off your own body (or a dirty old man's body, if you don't have any of your own)?

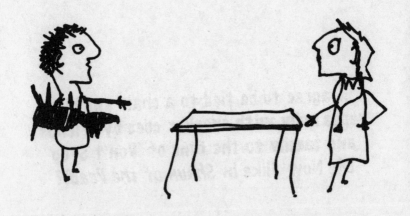

... TAKE A STUFFED, DEAD DOG WITH YOU TO A VET'S SURGERY AND SIT IN THE WAITING ROOM STROKING IT AND SAYING, 'POOR CEDRIC, HE'S GETTING AWFUL STIFF AND SLUGGISH IN HIS OLD AGE'?

... run up to a burly bouncer and slap him with a big wet fish?

... give yourself a massive wedgie and wear the leg-holes of your underwear hoisted over your shoulders for a day?

FOR £250, WOULD YOU...

... go to a friend's wedding, pretend you have developed Tourette's and shout out obscenities all the way through the ceremony?

... steal a copper's helmet, then cup it over your crotch and yell 'Oh boy! I think I caught a live one!!'

... run a full marathon after
eating three fry-ups?

... commandeer your boss's phone and
send a message to their partner saying
that they are looking forward to a
good spanking when they get home?

... wet yourself in a public place then
dramatically shrug and say 'oops'?

... put a live earwig in each ear?

... go to a football match and sit in the home stand of you local team wearing a bikini made from the visiting team's away strip?

... walk into an upmarket spa and announce loudly to the receptionist, 'Can you slot me in for my usual back, sack and crack, please?'

... ask an adolescent boy with terrible acne if he will let you squeeze his spots for ten pence a go? If he agrees, you have to say 'Ooh, ooh, it's a big one!' in a sexual voice each time one pops.

... cover your entire body in duct tape?

... go to the beach on a scorching hot day wearing a latex catsuit with matching gimp mask?

... end each working day for a month by spontaneously bursting into song and interpretive dance, incorporating the events of your day into the lyrics and movements?

... wash every meal down with a pint of vegetable oil for a week?

... call the French president 'a silly little man' to his face and then ask for 'a go' on his wife?

... wallow in meat paste, roll around on some slices of bread then make sandwiches out of the meat-paste-smeared bread and serve them at your grandmother's birthday tea? You can't wash any remaining meat paste off yourself until after the party.

... HUNT AND KILL A DEER,
GUT IT, THEN CRAWL
INSIDE IT FOR WARMTH?

... dress as a washroom attendant and spend a month touring your local pubs offering to perfume customers' undercarriages while they're taking a leak?

... sunbathe topless on the lawn outside your office for half an hour?

... stick photocopies of your arse to all the computer screens in your office, including your boss's, with the words, 'I know you want me' written at the top of the page?

... spend an hour in a sleeping bag with live cockroaches in it? You're not allowed to interfere with the insects – if one settles down in your arm pit for the hour or decides to explore your arse crack, there's nothing you can do about it.

... post a video of yourself waxing
your bikini line on YouTube?

... get a mahogany all-over spray tan, with
the words 'Insert cock here' bleached out
on your butt? You have to spend an hour
sunbathing front down on a busy beach.

... take a piss in a bin on the high
street in full daylight, whilst out
shopping with your mum?

WOULD YOU PiERCE THE BRIDGE OF YOUR NOSE WiTH A NEEDLE MAKiNG SURE iT GOES ALL THE WAY THROUGH FOR £256.21?

... staple your cleavage together?

... set your mobile phone to vibrate, shove it up your bum and get a friend to ring it?

FOR £500, WOULD YOU...

... hammer a nail under your thumbnail?

... refrain from washing for three months, claiming that you think the smell is sexy when anyone comments?

... get a Gary Glitter tattoo in a prominent place?

... live on a diet of various
animal penises for a week?

—

... get dragged at the back of a
truck Indiana Jones style for half
a mile? You could wear his leather
jacket and hat if you wanted.

—

... put up a ten-foot high poster of yourself
in your local town centre with the words
'you know me... I'm a wanker' printed
underneath? It has to up for a week.

... SHAVE HALF YOUR HAIR AND FACIAL HAIR AND KEEP ONE SIDE CLEAN SHAVEN FOR A WEEK?

... nail a pig's heart (from a butcher) to your boss's office door? You can bag an extra £200 if you succeed in convincing your boss it was the work of a colleague.

... let a crab clamp one of your nipples with its claw?

... go out to dinner in a Michelin star restaurant and puke up over your meal before eating it, saying you're following the new celebrity fad diet?

... let your toenails grow for one year, then cut them and have the clippings made into a necklace and insist on wearing it at all times for a month, claiming it is part of your tribe's cultural heritage?

... skip around a busy roundabout in broad daylight stark naked singing Chesney Hawkes' 'The One and Only!', waggling your genitals as you went?

... lick a dog's bum hole?

WOULD YOU TREAD iN A STiLL WARM PiLE OF DOG SHiT, CLEAN iT OFF YOUR SHOE WiTH YOUR TOOTHBRUSH AND THEN USE THE TOOTHBRUSH TO BRUSH YOUR TEETH FOR A WEEK AFTERWARDS FOR £543.26?

... fill a sink in a nightclub with the beverage of your choice, and drink it through a straw that's been wiped round the toilet?

... tell your mum you're cooking her a lovely roast then stuff the chicken with shit and glaze the roasted potatoes with wee? She must have at least one bite of each thing.

... go on the beat for a day dressed
as a policeman, but naked from the
waist down, and introduce yourself
to passers-by as PC Pervert?

... drink a shot of your best friend's blood?

FOR £1,000,

WOULD YOU...

... get naked, smear jam on your private parts and then let 30 wasps loose in the same room as you for half an hour?

... use a hedgehog as a sponge while you shower?

... spend an afternoon trapped in a lift with a skunk?

... put your head in between the buttocks of an old man – who has just eaten four tins of baked beans and a cauliflower curry and has extreme flatulence – for one hour?

––––––

... shit yourself at a sell-out concert? If you hear someone say 'God, what's that smell?' you have to shout 'That was me and I'm cool with it!'

... SIT ON THE SIDE OF THE ROAD EATING ROADKILL? JUST FIVE BITES. IN FULL VIEW OF ALL THE TRAFFIC.

... keep a haddock down your
pants for a week?

... drink the water out of a fish tank
that hasn't been cleaned for a month?

... go without sleep for a fortnight?
Every time you nod off a burly old
man will bang a cymbal near your
head and slap you in the face.

... have someone hit you repeatedly and continuously with a spoon on the same part of your body for three weeks?

... get baptised and when the water touches your head shout 'Ahhhh it burns, ah geez this fucking burns, what have you done?!' in front of the entire church congregation?

WOULD YOU HAVE A FULL BODY WAX AND MAINTAIN IT FOR SIX MONTHS FOR £1,500?

... wallpaper your dining room with used toilet paper, then invite your in-laws round for dinner?

... stick a used sanitary pad to the back of your skirt and walk around until someone points it out, then say: 'Oh, I wondered where that had got to! Lucky you spotted it – it's my last one!' and shove it back down the front of your skirt?

... climb Ben Nevis wearing only a loin cloth?

... MAIL YOURSELF TO SCOTLAND? YOU WOULD BE TIED IN BUT SUPPLIED WITH FOOD AND WATER. HOWEVER, THEY MAY PACK YOU UPSIDE DOWN...

... find a sloppy, fresh dog poo on the pavement, get down on all fours and give it a good old sniff, then lie down and rub your back on it, wiggling your legs in the air while barking frantically?

... would you watch *Transformers 2* over and over again, night and day, with two hours' sleep a night, for a whole month?

FOR £2,500,
WOULD YOU...

... visit your local wildlife park dressed as an emu, gain access to the big birds' enclosure and make as many attempts as possible to 'mount' one before the wardens tranquilise you?

... let someone's granny pull out all your pubic hairs with a pair of tweezers?

... ride a children's pedal tractor along the hard shoulder of the M1?

... do one-pot cooking in the bowl of a train toilet and serve it in baps for anyone who's interested?

... go to a modern art gallery, strip, cover yourself in gold paint and pose without moving for three days?

... swap wardrobes with Lady Gaga for a month, whether you're male or female?

... write your own obituary and post it in the local paper complete with your home telephone number? You get an extra £10 for each person that calls to pay their respects.

... storm into a bank with a strip of hotdogs strapped around your waist and shout, 'Anybody move and I'll set this thing off – these are one hundred per cent German frankfurters!'?

... BE BURiED ALiVE iN A COFFiN FOR TWO DAYS? YOU WiLL HAVE ENOUGH AiR AND PROViSiONS. YOU CAN UP THE ANTE TO £5,000 iF YOU LET FIVE RATS ACCOMPANY YOU, OR TO £1 MiLLiON iF YOU DO iT AT THE SAME TiME AS 999 OTHER PEOPLE, KNOWiNG THAT ONE OF YOU WiLL GET LEFT DOWN THERE TO DiE.

... skinny dip for ten minutes in crocodile-infested waters?

—

... turn up at your boss's house to perform a strippergram? When they recognise you yell, 'You see what your shit pay has reduced me to? I have a family to feed for chrissakes!!!!'?

... wear revealing shorts and perform five 'accidental' crotch shots a month for six months?

... get completely wankered on a mixture of Sambuca, tequila and red wine. Then, when you've got the hangover from hell the next day, head to the fairground and eat a whole tub of mayonnaise with anchovies in it whilst whizzing round on the waltzers. If it makes you throw up, you have to smear the sick all over yourself and roll around on the ground in front of the ride wailing: 'Why? Why?!!! WHY?!!!!'

... put live maggots in your hair and leave them there until they hatch into flies?

... take the supporting slot for Radiohead and play a half-hour set armed only with a flute, a banjo, a kazoo and a snare drum? Every other person in the sold-out venue has a rotten tomato; every time you get hit by one, £100 is deducted.

... stay in bed for six months with the curtains drawn? You will be on fully paid leave and have access to whatever home entertainment system you want – but absolutely no movement away from the bed is allowed, not even to stretch your legs, go to the toilet or wash.

FOR **£5,000,**
WOULD YOU...

... tell your boss to 'shove his poxy job'?

... stand up during the speeches at a friend's wedding and announce that you had slept with the bride/groom?

... have your whole body tattooed
in camouflage print?

... marry a really ugly, smelly person
for a week? You must consummate the
marriage and know them in the biblical
sense for at least an hour every day.

... GO SNORKELLING in
A SEWAGE PLANT?

... spend a year without using deodorant, soap or shampoo?

... auction yourself as a slave on eBay? If someone buys you, you must serve out two weeks' enslavement.

... breed hundreds of mosquitoes, then spend a week sleeping every night in an enclosed room with them?

... tell your parents that you have AIDS and let them believe it for a week?

FOR £10,000, WOULD YOU...

... repeatedly try to touch Mike Tyson's nuts until he flips out and punches you? There is an extra £10,000 if he eats your ear and an extra £20,000 if he rapes you.

... spend a week in a public toilet with only unflushed loo water to drink? You will be given a tuna mayo sandwich to eat each day to keep your energy levels up. If someone decides to use the toilet you can't stop them, but do remind them not to flush.

WOULD YOU CHANGE YOUR NAME BY DEED POLL TO PETER PHILE FOR £12,500?

... appear on a naturist version of *Come Dine With Me* and invite all your work colleagues to watch the episode at your house?

... rub one off in the back seat of your nan's car while she is driving?

... eat a chocolate eclair that has had the cream replaced with tortoise sperm?

... drive your car into a lamp post at 50 mph? You can use whatever excuse you like when you call the emergency services to report the incident.

... get married to a bridge, fire engine, urinal or other inanimate object?

FOR £25,000,

WOULD YOU...

... get bitten by a poisonous snake knowing you will only be given anti-venom at the last possible moment?

... touch a heated up soldering iron to your tongue for ten seconds?

... make a porn film with your partner, complete with authentic packaging, and put it on the shelf at your local video store?

WOULD YOU WALK INTO A POLICE STATION DRESSED AS A CARTOON PIG IN A POLICEMAN'S UNIFORM AND ENQUIRE WHETHER THERE ARE ANY JOB VACANCIES FOR £26,532?

... strip naked, wrap yourself in cling film and infiltrate the House of Commons during Prime Minister's Questions?

... dress as a lamb chop, cover yourself in the meaty juices from a roast dinner and then hug a lion?

... kill the family pet and
serve it for dinner?

... have your bum hole stitched
shut for two weeks?

FOR £50,000,
WOULD YOU...

... let a tapeworm live in your body for six months?

... sleep with someone three times your age?

... have all your teeth removed by a professional dentist? Or for £250,000, have them removed by a builder with a claw hammer? Either way you can have free false teeth put in afterwards.

FOR £50,000, WOULD YOU...

... HAVE AN UDDER GRAFTED TO YOUR CHEST AND, WHEN REVEALING iT TO YOUR FRiENDS, EXPLAIN THAT YOU SHALL HENCEFORTH BE KNOWN AS UDDERMAN OR UDDERWOMAN?

... have a colonic irrigation and drink the used arse water afterwards?

... exfoliate from top to toe with a cheese grater, then take a dip in the sea?

... have your legs strapped together and hop everywhere for three months?

FOR £100,000,

WOULD YOU...

... cross dress to go to work and ask everyone to call you Natasha (men) or Bruce (women) for a year? An extra £50,000 will be awarded if you keep this up outside of work.

... take hallucinogenic mushrooms every other day for a year? You have to wear a gnome's costume and carry a fishing rod around with you.

... go on prime-time television as the star of a half-hour documentary entitled The Man With the World's Smallest Penis (or The Woman with the Biggest, Flappiest Vagina)?

... HAVE YOUR TESTICLES
REMOVED AND MADE
INTO EARRINGS?

... have your ear removed by a surgeon?
For an extra £100,000, hack it off
yourself with a rusty blunt bread knife.

... take a laxative and a Viagra before a
meeting with your company's directors
and wait to see which one kicks in first?

... base jump from the top of the
Burj Khalifa building in Dubai?

FOR £250,000, WOULD YOU...

... have your appendix removed, cooked to perfection by a celebrity chef, then eat it?

... live underwater in a diving bell for six months?

... have your internal organs tattooed on the outside of your body?

WOULD YOU DRIVE AT SPEED UP TO A TOWER BRIDGE AND PERFORM A *DUKES OF HAZZARD* STYLE JUMP ACROSS TO THE OTHER SIDE JUST AS IT WAS BEING RAISED FOR £450,800?

... have your knees reversed in an operation and pretend you were Mr Tummus from *The Lion, the Witch and the Wardrobe* for a year? You must also knit your own scarf to complete the look.

———

... jump into the gorilla pit of a zoo? It takes as long as it takes to be rescued.

FOR £500,000,

WOULD YOU...

... confess to being the murderer in an unsolved crime and stand trial in the case?

—

... swim from Geyser Rock to Dyer Island off the coast of South Africa, crossing the channel otherwise known as 'Shark Alley' due to its high population of great white sharks?

... HAVE PLASTIC SURGERY ON YOUR FOREHEAD TO MAKE IT LOOK LIKE A PAIR OF FULSOME BUTTOCKS?

... swallow seven shaved Barbie doll heads and then go to your local hospital for an X-ray?

... have a tattoo on your forehead saying 'I used to have a dick here' for the rest of your life?

FOR £1 MILLION, WOULD YOU...

... chop two fingers off your non-dominant hand? One of them must be an index finger.

... sprawl out in the road and let a steam roller crush your legs?

... camp out in a refuse tip for a whole year? You must survive using only things that you find at the tip for food and shelter.

... go into a witness relocation program and live as a goatherd in the outer reaches of Siberia for 20 years?

... lie out in the blazing desert sun with no sun block on for 72 hours?

WHAT WOULD YOU DO FOR SiLLY MONEY?

Would you let yourself be cloned enough times to fill every traffic warden's job in Britain, so that you inspired fear and suspicion in every person you met, for £2,000,000?

Would you knowingly allow a candiru fish to wedge itself in your urethra for £2,500,000?

Would you chloroform your nan for £3,000,000? You can't give her any warning. Afterwards it's up to you whether you split the cash with her.

Would you agree to have your house demolished and a swamp made in its place for £3,500,000? You must live in a rotting hollow tree in the middle of it, with no overhead shelter for at least six months.

WOULD YOU HAVE YOUR LEG AMPUTATED, REPLACED WITH A WOODEN PEG, THEN CHANGE YOUR NAME TO LONG JOHN FISH BOTTOM FOR £4,000,000?

Would you have your tongue removed and sewn onto one of your cheeks for £4,500,000?

Would you go to prison for ten years for £5,000,000?

Would you spend every night for the rest of your life sleeping in a glass cube suspended above the River Thames for £10,000,000?

Have you enjoyed this book?
If so, why not write a review
on your favourite website?

Thanks very much for buying
this Summersdale book.

www.summersdale.com